A DVD-based study series
Study Guide

JESUS
Man, Messiah, or More?

A DVD-based study series
Study Guide

JESUS

Man, Messiah, or More?

With Mart De Haan and the
Institute for Biblical Research Jesus Study Group

Sixteen Lessons for Group Exploration

Feeding the Soul with the Word of God

The DayLight Bible Studies are based on programs produced by
Day of Discovery, a Bible-teaching TV series of RBC Ministries.

© 2010 by Discovery House Publishers

Discovery House Publishers is affiliated with RBC Ministries,
Grand Rapids, Michigan.

Requests for permission to quote from this book should be directed to:
Permissions Department
Discovery House Publishers
P.O. Box 3566
Grand Rapids, MI 49501

All Scripture quotations, unless otherwise indicated, are taken from the
HOLY BIBLE, NEW INTERNATIONAL VERSION®. NIV®
Copyright © 1973, 1978, 1984 by Biblica, Inc. ™
Used by permission of Zondervan.
All rights reserved.

Study questions by Andrew Sloan
Interior design by Sherri L. Hoffman
Cover design by Jeremy Culp
Cover photo by istockphoto

ISBN: 978-1-57293-397-2

Printed in the United States of America

10 11 12 13 / / 10 9 8 7 6 5 4 3 2 1

CONTENTS

Introduction: One Incredible Story — 7

SESSION 1
Capernaum: The Birthplace of Christianity — 9

SESSION 2
Jesus: Man of Authority — 16

SESSION 3
Jesus and the Big Question — 23

SESSION 4
A Case for Truth — 29

SESSION 5
Jesus Enters Jerusalem — 36

SESSION 6
Palm Sunday — 43

SESSION 7
The Temple Controversy — 51

SESSION 8
What Was Jesus Doing? — 58

SESSION 9
Jesus and the Last Supper — 66

SESSION 10
Jesus Introduces His Death   74

SESSION 11
The Examination of Jesus   82

SESSION 12
Objections to the Examination Story   89

SESSION 13
Who Killed Jesus and Why?   96

SESSION 14
The Reality of the Crucifixion Accounts   103

SESSION 15
What Happened to Jesus' Body?   109

SESSION 16
What About the Empty Tomb?   116

INTRODUCTION

One Incredible Story

You've got to admit it: This is one truly remarkable story.

A baby was born without a human father. He grew up in poverty and obscurity in an out-of-the-way town in Israel. He became a carpenter, learning the trade from his dad. When this man turned 30 years old, he began to do miraculous things such as turning water into wine, healing sick people, making storms go away, and even bringing dead people back to life.

He went against everything the religious leaders of the day said was right. He broke their rules. He disrupted their temple activities. He even ended up calling them names and pronouncing woes upon them. So the religionists had this person arrested, and then they questioned him before turning him over to the governmental authorities. They had the man killed for claiming to be a king.

But that's when the story really gets crazy—where it surpasses the remarkable and starts edging toward the incredible.

This man didn't stay dead.

Three days after the government killed this supposed criminal about whom its leading official could find no wrong, citizens of the city and surrounding communities saw the man walking around talking to people.

This kind of thing doesn't happen to just anybody. And some people think it happened to nobody. These folks would like to conclude that this whole Jesus of Nazareth thing was a huge hoax—a meticulously created tale made up by some uneducated fishermen and craftsmen in the first century. These skeptics would like to think that the worldwide faith called Christianity is not provable and therefore not to be believed.

Yet there are many others who stand on the other side of that line—men and women who have studied the evidence of history, archaeology, manuscript studies, and biblical scholarship and have concluded that Jesus did all of those things mentioned above. They firmly and with intellectual honesty think that Jesus Christ is exactly who the Bible says He was and is.

One group of such scholars is called the Institute for Biblical Research, which is made up of people who have spent their adult lives examining the evidence for the reliability of Scripture. These scholars have each compiled an impressive array of credentials that verify their ability to dig into the evidence and come to intelligent conclusions. Each has written books on the subjects at hand—and each is considered a top expert in his area of expertise.

Mart De Haan and the crew of the television program *Day of Discovery* convened these scholars in Jerusalem to seek their help in answering one of the most vital questions of all: What is the evidence that Jesus Christ was indeed who the Bible says He was and that He really did what the Bible says He did? Mart and the scholars traveled to some of the most important locations in Israel to talk about these key issues.

- They went to Capernaum to talk about Jesus' miracles.
- They went to Caesarea Philippi to discuss the answers to Jesus' question of His disciples: "Who do you say I am?"
- They ended up in Jerusalem to examine Jesus' triumphal entry, His cleansing of the temple, His burial, and His resurrection. In each study, Mart questions the men as would any seeking person—digging from them the evidence and the proofs that help us solidify the veracity of the biblical stories.

The New Testament and the stories it contains can stand on their own. In a world of skepticism and even cynicism, there is abundant evidence to believe that Jesus the man was indeed Jesus the Messiah—and so much more. It may seem like an incredible story—but as you'll see from studying along with the scholars in this series, it has great credibility.

—Dave Branon
Editor

SESSION 1

Capernaum: The Birthplace of Christianity

DAYLIGHT PREVIEW

A Scholarly Approach

More often than we would like to think, the Christian faith is met with skepticism by its critics. Often people who discount Christianity seek to reduce the biblical core of our belief system to mythology—suggesting that it was all an elaborate, made-up story. That's why it is important to have men like Dr. Darrell Bock and his colleagues in the Institute for Biblical Research Jesus Study Group, who are willing to dedicate their professional lives to taking a closer, more critical look at the evidence. This group of scholars spent a decade sifting through the archaeology and the sources and the histories to see if the Bible story can stand up to good research. As they visit one of the most famous archaeological sites in the little town of Capernaum, they'll help you realize that the evidence is overwhelmingly in favor of the authenticity of God's Book, the Bible.

COME TOGETHER

Icebreaker Questions

1. On a scale of 1 to 10, how much did you enjoy history classes when you were growing up?

2. Can you recall being part of a study group during your educational journey? How did you feel about that experience?

3. Jesus' ministry headquarters was in the region of the Sea of Galilee known yet today for its farming and fishing. Which are you better at—farming (gardening; taking care of plants) or fishing?

4. Have you ever visited a synagogue? If so, what was that experience like?

FINDING DAYLIGHT

Experience the Video

Feel free to jot down Video Notes as you watch the presentation by Mart De Haan and the Jesus Study Group. Use the space below for those notes.

———————— **VIDEO NOTES** ————————

Questions about Jesus

The approach of the scholars

The town of Capernaum

An ancient synagogue

The synagogue's archaeology and significance

The scholars and Capernaum

Jesus' ministry and Judaism

What the scholars are doing

The activities of Jesus

Mart's summation

WALKING IN THE DAYLIGHT

Discussion Time

---DISCOVER GOD'S WORD---

Discussion/Application Questions

1. Speaking for the Jesus Study Group, Dr. Craig A. Evans says that the approach taken by the group toward Jesus of Nazareth "is the same approach we would take if we were interested in the historical Alexander the Great or the historical Julius Caesar."

   How do you feel about that approach? How realistic is it for Christians to take that approach objectively?

2. The Synoptic Gospels (Matthew, Mark, and Luke) show that Capernaum and the surrounding region of the Galilee was the birthplace of the ministry of Jesus and therefore of Christianity. Note this as you read Mark 1:14–39.

   a. Why is it important that we recognize that the gospel accounts are describing a real time and place when they say that Jesus, a rabbi from Nazareth, entered the community of Capernaum and amazed His Jewish countrymen by the way He opened up their Scriptures?

b. Why is it important that we realize that Christianity is not so much a break with Judaism as it is something that is rooted in Judaism—and that Jesus really didn't come to form a distinctly new religion?

3. **Commenting on Mark 1:23–28, Dr. Evans notes that Jesus' casting out a demon was a tangible demonstration of the power of God defeating the power of Satan.**

   What was the significance of that demonstration then? What is its significance for us today?

4. **In response to Mart De Haan's question about the distinction between the old and new covenants, Dr. Darrell L. Bock points out that the new covenant is a part of the very Scriptures that are at the heart of Judaism. In that light, read Jeremiah 31:31–34.**

   In what sense is this "new covenant" both new and rooted in God's long-term plan?

5. **The first session of this series starts with the note that this group of scholars has been working for ten years to show that a person doesn't have to begin by believing that the Bible is the Word of God in order to discover who Jesus really was.**

Reflecting on your own life: What are your beliefs and assumptions about the Bible, particularly regarding God's role in it and its authority?

Reflecting on your own life: What are your beliefs and assumptions about Jesus, particularly in regard to the historical accuracy of the gospel accounts about Him?

Reflecting on your own life: Which came first—your beliefs and assumptions about the Bible or your beliefs and assumptions about Jesus?

DAYLIGHT ON PRAYER

A Time to Share

1. What drew you to this study about Jesus?

2. How could the group support you in prayer in regard to your relationship with Christ?

3. In what other ways can the group support you in prayer today?

14   JESUS: MAN, MESSIAH, OR MORE?

DAYLIGHT AHEAD

Did you ever wonder why Jesus did so many miracles? In Session 2, you can sit in the ancient synagogue at Capernaum with Mart De Haan and a collection of noted biblical scholars and discover why Jesus cast out demons, raised the dead, and helped the lame to walk. Listen as these men who have spent years studying Jesus' life and times explain what was behind the Savior's great humanitarian acts.

SESSION 2

Jesus: Man of Authority

 DAYLIGHT PREVIEW

Any Questions?

As Jesus walked the dusty roads of Israel healing people and casting out demons, He was not putting on a show. He was answering important questions about His identity and His role on earth. That's why when John was in prison and sent a question to Jesus about who He was, the Savior replied, "Go and tell John the things which you hear and see" (John 11:4). As the scholars of the Institute for Biblical Research Jesus Study Group begin to point out, Jesus' actions were clear indications that He had come into the world to do something no one else could do—fulfill and complete the law of Judaism. His miracles were verifications of His authority to do that.

COME TOGETHER

Icebreaker Questions

1. Can you remember a teacher who was really able to grab your attention?

2. We see in this session that Jesus did some things that were out of the ordinary. Do you see yourself as more of a conformist or a nonconformist?

16 JESUS: MAN, MESSIAH, OR MORE?

3. The scholars in our study had an inside joke about Dr. Robert Webb and his book on John the Baptist. Does your family have any inside jokes? Can you disclose one?

 FINDING DAYLIGHT

Experience the Video

Feel free to jot down Video Notes as you watch the presentation by Mart De Haan and the Jesus Study Group. Use the space below for those notes.

──────────── **VIDEO NOTES** ────────────

The value of Jesus' miracles

Questions about Jesus as Messiah

The Sabbath controversy

Opposition to Jesus: Why?

The authority of Jesus

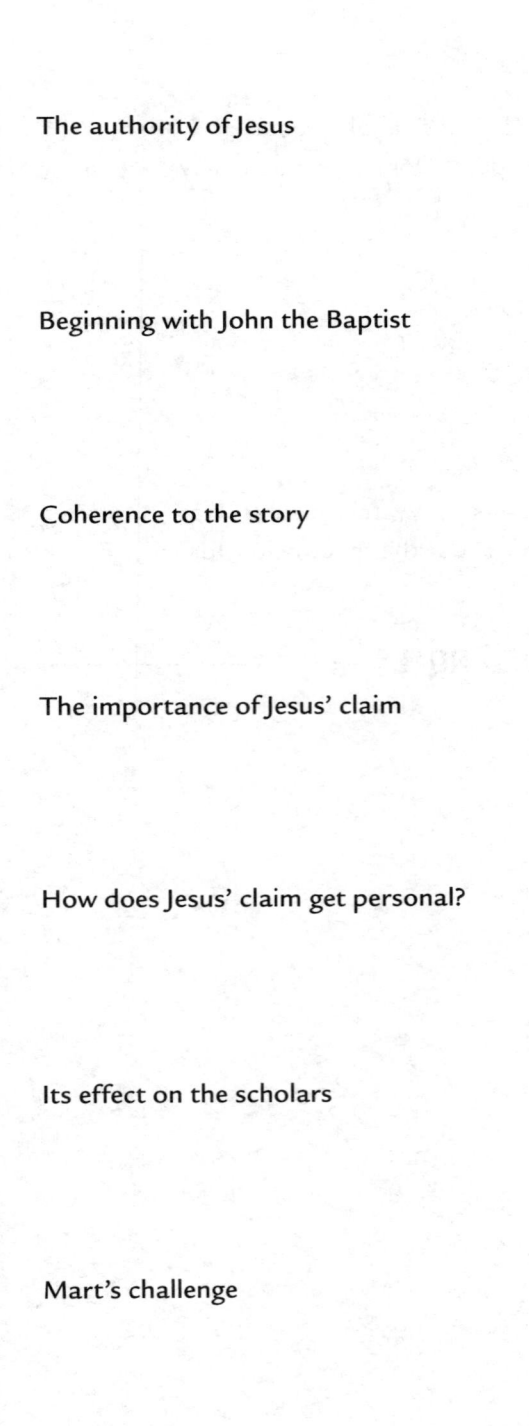

Beginning with John the Baptist

Coherence to the story

The importance of Jesus' claim

How does Jesus' claim get personal?

Its effect on the scholars

Mart's challenge

WALKING IN THE DAYLIGHT

Discussion Time

DISCOVER GOD'S WORD

Discussion/Application Questions

1. As the Jesus Study Group scholars have shown, Capernaum and the surrounding region of the Galilee was the birthplace of the ministry of Jesus and therefore of Christianity. Read Mark 1:21–28.

    Why was Jesus' authority so striking to people?

2. Dr. Craig A. Evans points out that Jesus didn't perform miracles simply for their own sake. Jesus wasn't putting on a show; His miracles had a greater purpose. In that regard, read Matthew 11:1–6.

    a. Did Jesus actually answer John's question?

    b. What did Jesus' words imply about His identity and about the purpose of His miracles?

3. The scholars note that the background of Jesus' actions and words was found in Isaiah 61, which people in the Jewish world would have immediately understood. Read Isaiah 61:1–2.

How was Jesus alluding to this well-known passage in reference to His being the Messiah?

4. This session looks at the so-called "Sabbath controversy"—the dispute caused by Jesus' healing of people on the Sabbath. Read Matthew 12:1–14.

   a. What does Jesus' bold claim to be "Lord of the Sabbath" say about His authority? About His relationship to Judaism?

   b. How did the Jewish religious leaders react to Jesus' claim? Why?

5. Dr. Darrell L. Bock states that our culture, for the most part, says that we have a high regard and respect for Jesus Christ—"that He's a terrifically important person, that He's one of the greats of all time, that if we had a religious hall of fame, we'd put Him in there. He might even get the most votes!"

   Why does putting Jesus in the religious hall of fame with a whole bunch of other people miss the point of the unique claims Jesus was making about himself?

6. In response to Mart De Haan's question about how Jesus' claims become personal, Dr. Bock says they do so because they deal with life and death and with the purpose for why we live and how we

should live. Dr. Bock then notes that "all those questions end up being wrapped up in what it means to come under the rule of the living God."

What is that "rule" like?

Reflecting on your own life: How have you experienced the "rule of the living God" in your own life?

7. **Dr. Grant R. Osborne says, in essence, that he's a Christian first and a scholar second.**

   Reflecting on your own life: Does being a Christian take precedence over any other self-identity or self-understanding in your life?

   Reflecting on your own life: What are the biggest challenges for you in that regard?

8. **Dr. Michael J. Wilkins observes that people often say they wish they could have had the opportunity that the original disciples had to be with Jesus.**

   Reflecting on your own life: Can you relate to that desire?

Reflecting on your own life: Do you also share Dr. Wilkins' sense of having a daily discipleship walk with Jesus—the privilege of being in a relationship with Him every single day?

DAYLIGHT ON PRAYER

A Time to Share

1. At the end of this session, Dr. Bock mentions that a lot of people feel very disconnected from their world, as they feel lonely, alienated, and estranged. When has that been the most true for you?

2. Dr. Bock concludes by saying, "Jesus' goal is to get inside of us and reconnect us to where we ought to be. And in the process of doing that you find yourself and you find the living God." How satisfied are you with your sense of connection?

3. What other prayer requests do you have to share with the group?

DAYLIGHT AHEAD

From Capernaum, Mart and some members of the Jesus Study Group travel north to the ancient ruins of the city of Caesarea Philippi. It was in this region that Jesus and His disciples took part in one of the most significant conversations of Jesus' life on earth. The geography, the archaeology, and the discussion of Jesus' time here with His disciples make this a fascinating visit to northern Israel.

SESSION 3

Jesus and the Big Question

DAYLIGHT PREVIEW

Putting Peter on the Spot

As Jesus and His closest friends traveled through the region of Caesarea Philippi, He asked them a penetrating, valuable question. While they all had a chance to respond, it was Peter's response that garnered the most attention then—and still attracts our attention now. Boldly and seemingly without hesitation, the former fisherman said, "You are the Christ." As stunning as Peter's answer had to be, what was even more startling was Jesus' response to it. Because He had something in mind that no one else could understand, He responded in a way that while seeming harsh to us was necessary. The Jesus Study Group helps us understand what was behind this exchange.

COME TOGETHER

Icebreaker Questions

1. How good were you at keeping a secret when you were a kid? How about now?

2. What is the biggest rock or mountain you have ever climbed?

3. If you are married, where and how did you—or your future spouse— "pop the question"?

FINDING DAYLIGHT

Experience the Video

Feel free to jot down Video Notes as you watch the presentation by Mart De Haan and the Jesus Study Group. Use the space below for those notes.

──────────── **VIDEO NOTES** ────────────

Caesarea Philippi

Peter's statement

New Testament scholars: Their task

Dr. Paul Wright and the geography of Caesarea Philippi

Jesus' response to Peter

Peter and the rock

Why did Jesus wait until now to ask His question?

Is the story true or made up?

"Tipping point" in Jesus' life

Jesus' response to Peter: Don't tell

How Jesus introduced His kingdom

 WALKING IN THE DAYLIGHT

Discussion Time

---—— DISCOVER GOD'S WORD ——---

Discussion/Application Questions

1. The scene in Matthew 16 occurs about two and a half years into Jesus' ministry. People are amazed by His teaching and miracles. Everyone in Galilee knows that something significant is happening.

Jesus is considered a great teacher, a great prophet, and maybe even more than that. In light of this background, read Matthew 16:13-14.

What do these speculations indicate about the popular views of Jesus' identity? (Note: Matthew 14:1-12 records that John the Baptist had recently been beheaded by Herod Antipas, who conjectured that Jesus was John the Baptist raised from the dead.)

2. **Now read Matthew 16:15-16, the pivotal verses in this passage. Peter's "confession," or declaration, was that Jesus is the Messiah. Christians certainly believed that after Jesus' lifetime. But some scholars think that Peter's statement was too clear and too bold at this point, and therefore the early church must have written it back into the account some years later.**

How logical and convincing do you find this view?

3. **Continue looking at this story by reading Matthew 16:17-19.**

What do Jesus' words in verse 17 add to the significance of Peter's confession and to the question of the historicity, or authenticity, of this story?

4. **There has been much discussion and debate about the meaning of this "rock" upon which Jesus will build His church. Archaeologist Paul Wright says, "I find it interesting that, irrespective of the theological discussion and the historic discussion, Jesus is calling Peter (and *petros* means "rock," of course) under the shadow of the might-**

iest rock in this land—a massive mountain. It's a kind of a rock that provides strength and shelter and security—essentially everything necessary for life: water, soil, building materials, strength, and security. If the church isn't that, I don't know what it is."

How does Dr. Wright's association of Jesus' words in verse 18 with their setting in the area of the massive Mount Hermon affect your view of them?

5. **Now Jesus turns His attention from Peter to all of the twelve disciples. Read Matthew 16:20.**

   Why did Jesus want to keep His identity as the Messiah a secret?

6. **Read about Jesus' next communication with His disciples in Matthew 16:21.**

   a. Here we have Jesus' very first prediction that He will meet His demise in Jerusalem. What do the Jesus Study Group scholars mean when they say that this represents a major turning point in the gospel story?

   b. How does this help to explain the reason for the "messianic secret" found in verse 20?

7. In John's gospel we see the result of the people having the wrong understanding of Jesus as Messiah. Read the conclusion to Jesus' feeding of the five thousand in John 6:14–15.

   Do you think the disciples' understanding of Jesus as Messiah, at this point, was much different from the crowd's understanding?

DAYLIGHT ON PRAYER

A Time to Share

1. "What about you? Who do you say I am?" How has your understanding of Jesus and your relationship with Him developed and changed over time?

2. What is the cutting edge or growth point in your relationship with Christ now? How can the group support you in prayer?

3. What other concerns would you like to share with the group as you conclude with prayer?

DAYLIGHT AHEAD

Mart De Haan and his scholar friends are still in Caesarea Philippi discussing Peter's confession of faith. But they bring into the discussion a new wrinkle. Could it be that what Peter supposedly said on that day was an example of revisionist history? Could this story have been penciled into the pages of the Bible later—not as history but as an attempt to create history the way the new Christians wanted it to be? Find out how the Jesus Study Group responds to that possibility in Session 4 of this study.

SESSION 4

A Case for Truth

DAYLIGHT PREVIEW

Rewriting History

It's easy to see how it can be done. In fact, we can often see it in history books of our day. What historians of 40 years ago put in textbooks of American history, for instance, is not what historians of today put in the texts. Perhaps someone has a different agenda, so the stories are told with a different slant. Could that have happened with the Bible? Could the writers of this Book have decided that they needed to make the story stronger in the favor of Christianity—and thus enhanced Peter's answer to Jesus' question? That's what Mart De Haan and the Jesus Study Group scholars are discussing in this session of their study of Jesus.

COME TOGETHER

Icebreaker Questions

1. Dr. Michael Wilkins uses his middle initial, "J," which stands for James, as a humorous illustration. What is your middle name? How did your parents choose it, and how do you feel about it?

2. In this story, Peter needed to be rebuked by Jesus for his own good. How often did you have that need when you were growing up?

3. This was surely an embarrassment for Peter. Can you share one of your most embarrassing moments?

FINDING DAYLIGHT

Experience the Video

Feel free to jot down Video Notes as you watch the presentation by Mart De Haan and the Jesus Study Group. Use the space below for those notes.

──────────── **VIDEO NOTES** ────────────

Did Peter really make that declaration?

The standard of embarrassment

Using academic criteria

Why go to Caesarea Philippi?

What to say to the questioning person

Dr. Wilkins' story and Jesus

Power and the gospel

Peter's declaration and us

Mart's challenge

WALKING IN THE DAYLIGHT

Discussion Time

---**DISCOVER GOD'S WORD**---

Discussion/Application Questions

1. **Review this important story about Peter's confession, or declaration, by reading Matthew 16:13–22.**

    a. What future path would Peter, the other disciples, and the Jewish people in general want Jesus to take?

    b. What path did God have set out for Jesus?

2. **Now read Jesus' words to Peter in Matthew 16:23.**

    a. How would you have felt if Jesus spoke these words to you?

    b. Why do you think Jesus used such strong language? Do you think Jesus spoke so sternly not only for the sake of Peter and the other disciples but also in part for His own sake?

c. Why do the Jesus Study Group scholars believe Peter's embarrassment verifies the historicity, or authenticity, of this story?

d. Do you agree with Dr. Darrell Bock's conclusion that the reason the story is there "is because it was there"? Explain.

3. **The Jesus Study Group scholars view the location of this story as quite significant.**

   a. Why should we expect Jesus to go south to Jerusalem to elicit a declaration of His "messiahship" rather to travel quite a distance north to Caesarea Philippi?

   b. Furthermore, why did Jesus choose this area that was not only outside of Israel but also filled with pagan religious associations?

   c. How do these circumstances convey, as Dr. Michael Wilkins says, that as Jesus comes here, "There's a declaration that these old dead gods that we find here—there's nothing to them"?

4. Peter is known for his foibles—for example, for sticking his foot in his mouth here and on other occasions; for quickly getting out of the boat to walk with Jesus on the water, until he noticed the wind and waves and started sinking; and especially for denying the Lord three times after He was arrested. But Peter is also known for his sincere desire to follow Jesus and for becoming the leader and spokesman for Jesus' followers both during and after His lifetime.

   Dr. Wilkins shares that he can identify with Peter: sometimes getting it right, sometimes getting it wrong (and acting like a jerk)—yet all the time on a journey with Jesus.

   Reflecting on your own life: How can you relate to Dr. Wilkins' feelings?

5. Jesus used this occasion to deliver a challenging message to His disciples. Read His words in Matthew 16:24–26.

   Dr. Darrell Bock points out that Peter had a grand portrait of who Jesus should be as he gave his confession. But Jesus responded, in essence, by saying, "The way I'm going to show the world what the way is, is not through a huge exaltation but through this self-sacrifice that I'm entering into. And you're going to walk down the same road with Me. And you will learn more about who you are [by] taking that path than you will in trying to seek glory and honor to yourself."

   Reflecting on your own life: What have you learned about yourself in your efforts to "come after" Jesus and follow His path of self-sacrifice?

   Reflecting on your own life: In what particular way do you sense Christ calling you now to deny yourself and take up your cross?

DAYLIGHT ON PRAYER

A Time to Share

1. Dr. Michael Burer points out that Peter's declaration, in a way, becomes a paradigm for our own faith. It always seems to be two steps forward, one step back, then two steps forward, and one step back. What direction are you currently moving in your journey of faith?

2. Spend some time praying for other items shared by members of your group: the spiritual welfare of others, concerns for others around the world, personal points of praise and prayer.

DAYLIGHT AHEAD

Mart and the scholars of the Jesus Study Group move south for this session of their examination of Jesus—all the way down past Capernaum and the Sea of Galilee to Jerusalem. They are visiting the Holy City to discuss another incident in Jesus' life that needs to be verified if His story is to be believed. That event is the triumphal entry of Jesus into Jerusalem. Join the men as they look for evidence that it really happened as the Bible says it did.

SESSION 5

Jesus Enters Jerusalem

DAYLIGHT PREVIEW

Re-examining the Triumphal Entry

It's been a part of Christian teaching for centuries—a favorite story that included animals, celebrations, joy, and Jesus. But are the events of what we call Palm Sunday based on history? Mart De Haan, along with a team of Bible scholars from the Institute for Biblical Research, takes a closer look at this event to see how the findings of history coordinate with the record of the biblical account. This re-examination of Scripture and history can help solidify this important event as historically true.

COME TOGETHER

Icebreaker Questions

1. Mart De Haan seems to have made a new friend, Peter the donkey. What is your all-time favorite pet?

2. Who is the most famous person you have seen in person? Was the setting a parade or some other context?

3. Dr. Darrell Bock points out that sometimes our first impressions of people are wrong. How prone are you to making quick assumptions about people? How accurate would you say your perceptions turn out to be?

36 JESUS: MAN, MESSIAH, OR MORE?

FINDING DAYLIGHT

Experience the Video

Feel free to jot down Video Notes as you watch the presentation by Mart De Haan and the Jesus Study Group. Use the space below for those notes.

---— **VIDEO NOTES** ———

Mart's new friend, Peter

Jesus' entrance into Jerusalem then and now

What do we do with the skeptics?

The tradition of receiving important people in Jerusalem

How the triumphal entrance is different

The Pharisees and Jesus at the triumphal entry

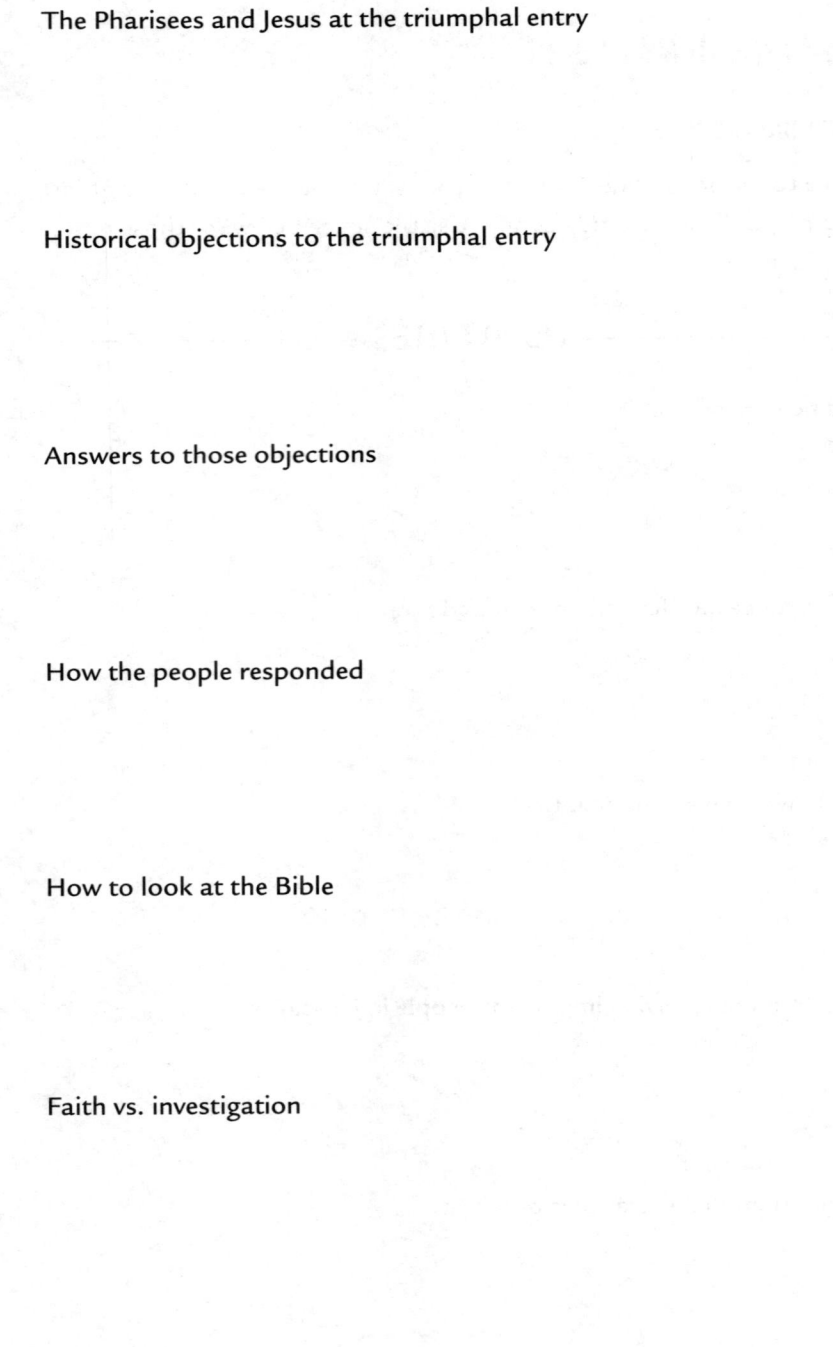

Historical objections to the triumphal entry

Answers to those objections

How the people responded

How to look at the Bible

Faith vs. investigation

WALKING IN THE DAYLIGHT

Discussion Time

---DISCOVER GOD'S WORD---

Discussion/Application Questions

1. The gospel of Mark begins its account of the triumphal entry with some background information, found in Mark 11:1–3. Jesus was traveling west from Jericho toward Jerusalem. Bethany was located on the eastern slope of the Mount of Olives, about two miles east of Jerusalem. Bethphage, a village even closer to Jerusalem, was likely the village to which Jesus sent two of His disciples.

   a. How do you think these two disciples felt about Jesus' instructions to go find a colt for Him?

   b. We don't know if "the Lord" Jesus spoke of in verse 3 referred to Jesus himself or to "the Lord God." In either case, what does this say about Jesus' perspective about this event?

2. We can see in Mark 11:4–10 how the story plays out. (Note: "Hosanna!" was a Hebrew expression that literally meant "Save!" but had become an exclamation of praise.)

   a. What are the indicators in this story that Jesus saw himself as the Messiah?

b. What are the indicators that the people in the crowd saw Jesus as the Messiah?

3. **The gospel of Luke adds an interesting piece of dialog at this point in the story. Turn to Luke 20:39–40.**

    a. What is the significance of the fact that the religious and political leaders of Israel were largely absent from Jesus' grand entry into the nation's capital—and that those who were there tried to throw a wet blanket on His entry?

    b. How do you suppose the Pharisees felt about Jesus' reply?

    c. What does Jesus' reply show about His attitude toward what the crowd was shouting?

4. **Dr. Brent Kinman notes that one objection to the claim that the triumphal entry actually occurred is that the biblical account is "too messianic." It portrays Jesus as coming as the Messiah; but since the Gospels present Jesus as hesitant to say publicly that He is the**

Messiah, His actual entry into Jerusalem couldn't have been what the Gospels describe.

How would you respond to that objection?

5. **A second objection is that if the triumphal entry is the big deal that the Gospels describe, surely the Romans would have come out and laid hands on this troublemaker Jesus.**

   How would you respond to that objection?

6. **Is it dangerous—or healthy—to ask if events like this in the Bible really happened?**

7. **Dr. Klyne Snodgrass says that the Jesus Study Group scholars "want people to investigate the faith. The faith will bear investigation. The Bible will take care of itself. One of the problems with modern-day Christianity is frequently Christians are too naïve about what they're doing. They need to be the most reflective people around."**

   a. How does such investigation fit with the old bumper sticker slogan: "God said it. I believe it. That settles it"?

b. How does such investigation fit with the command to "Love the Lord your God with all your heart and with all your soul and with all your mind and with all your strength" (Mark 12:30)?

DAYLIGHT ON PRAYER

A Time to Share

1. Dr. Snodgrass goes on to say that we need to take our faith seriously because that's the only kind of faith that's going to do us justice for the whole of life. How seriously are you taking your faith?

2. Are there any specific areas of your life that need help or prayer support? What other prayer requests would you like to share with the group?

DAYLIGHT AHEAD

It was one of the most poignant scenes in all of Scripture. Jesus—the Messiah, the fulfillment of Old Testament predictions—looks out over the city of Jerusalem and weeps for her. Just a few days before He is to face a cruel crucifixion, His heart breaks because of the spiritual blindness of the people. Mart De Haan and a group of Bible scholars visit the traditional site of Jesus' sadness to examine more deeply the events of Palm Sunday—looking for evidence of this event's authenticity.

SESSION 6

Palm Sunday

DAYLIGHT PREVIEW

Tradition or Truth?

All throughout Israel, buildings and monuments have been built to commemorate important events of biblical history. Churches have been constructed on or near the traditional sites of such events as Jesus' birth in Bethlehem, His Sermon on the Mount by the Sea of Galilee, and His crucifixion at Golgotha. But as Mart De Haan points out, when it comes to the actual events recorded in the Bible, we have to go past tradition and land on truth. Did the events we read about really happen as the Bible says they did? Did the events of Palm Sunday, for instance, happen as the Bible describes? These are key questions for all who trust in Jesus.

COME TOGETHER
Icebreaker Questions

1. What's the biggest celebration or "feast" you have ever participated in?

2. How interested are you in past or present royalty (for example, Britain's)?

3. How easily do you cry?

4. Have you ever marched in a parade? How about a Palm Sunday parade?

FINDING DAYLIGHT

Experience the Video

Feel free to jot down Video Notes as you watch the presentation by Mart De Haan and the Jesus Study Group. Use the space below for those notes.

———————————— VIDEO NOTES ————————————

Jesus wept over Jerusalem

The event: Answering the objections

Jesus' orchestration of the events

Other important events in Jesus' life

How the events converge: What is the picture?

What was happening that day?

    a. Jesus' claim

    b. It doesn't go well

Where does someone go with this?

The heart issue: Would you follow Jesus?

You make the call

WALKING IN THE DAYLIGHT

Discussion Time

DISCOVER GOD'S WORD
Discussion/Application Questions

1. The account of the triumphal entry in the gospel of John adds some interesting insights to that of the Synoptic Gospels (Matthew, Mark, and Luke), which have much in common with each other. Read John's version of the story in John 12:12–18.

    Two groups converge here. One group consisted of the twelve disciples and other followers of Jesus, many of whom had witnessed the raising of Lazarus in Bethany not long before this (see verse 17). The other group consisted of Jewish pilgrims who had come to Jerusalem to celebrate the Passover Feast (see verse 1)—many of whom undoubtedly had come from Galilee, where they had seen and heard Jesus, and/or had heard about Jesus raising Lazarus from the dead (see verse 18). This group came out of Jerusalem to meet Jesus and the other group as they approached the city (see verses 13 and 18).

    a. Read the response of the Pharisees who were present in verse 19. Although they clearly spoke in exaggerated terms, how did these Pharisees feel about what was happening?

    b. How was this a case of the religious leaders ironically speaking much more accurately (in other words, prophetically) than they realized? (See verses 20–21 and 32.)

c. John notes in verse 16 that he and the other disciples didn't realize the significance of this event and the Old Testament prophecies about it until after Jesus was "glorified" (through His death, resurrection, and exaltation). What does that say about the contention of some today that the triumphal entry didn't actually occur but was made up later by the Christian community?

2. **In verse 15 John quotes part of Zechariah 9:9, obviously viewing this scene as a fulfillment of that prophecy. Take a look at the complete context of Zechariah 9:9–10. (Note: The phrases "Daughter of Zion" and "Daughter of Jerusalem" are personifications of Jerusalem, the spiritual and political center of Israel.)**

   a. How is the donkey of verse 9 contrasted with the horse (or horses) of verse 10?

   b. What does the fact that a king riding a horse symbolized war while a king riding a donkey symbolized peace say about Jesus and His kingdom?

   c. What does the fact that David and his sons rode a donkey or mule (2 Samuel 16:2; 1 Kings 1:33) say about Jesus and His kingdom?

SESSION 6—Palm Sunday   47

3. Dr. Brent Kinman points out that Jesus clearly was intentionally presenting himself as Jerusalem's king, its rightful king.

   In light of the realities of the Roman Empire, why was this a profoundly provocative act?

4. Luke's account of the triumphal entry ends with a reference to the peace that Jerusalem could have known. Read Luke 19:41–44.

   a. These verses surely describe the Romans' destruction of Jerusalem in AD 70. How do you think scholars who doubt the historicity of the triumphal entry would feel about the prospect of Jesus actually having spoken these words?

   b. What did Jesus mean that Jerusalem did not recognize the time of God's "coming" or "visitation"?

   c. This is the second time Jesus is said to have wept. (The first was at Lazarus' tomb; John 11:35). What do Jesus' tears tell us about Him and about how He felt about Jerusalem?

5. Dr. Kinman notes that the triumphal entry "represents for Jerusalem a day of decision. Jesus comes; He's known; they understand about Him. And He says, 'Today's the day—you need to decide.' And what hangs in the balance is almost everything."

   Reflecting on your own life: In the past, how have you sensed Jesus calling you to make a decision in regard to following Him? In what way do you sense Jesus calling you to make a decision in regard to following Him now?

DAYLIGHT ON PRAYER

A Time to Share

Mart De Haan concludes this session by connecting Jesus' weeping over Jerusalem with the experience of modern-day Christians who come to Jerusalem to remember Palm Sunday. "When they come, they too shed tears: tears of gratitude for themselves, and tears of concern for those who still think of Jesus as simply a good man—rather than as the Messiah, the King and the Savior that the evidence of history shows Him to be."

1. How much can you relate to the notion of shedding tears of gratitude for what Christ has done for us? Spend time as a group thanking Him for this.

2. How much can you relate to the notion of shedding tears of concern for those who don't think of Jesus as the Messiah? Are there specific individuals or situations you would like the group to lift up in prayer?

DAYLIGHT AHEAD

One of the most surprising actions of Jesus' life was an event that took place on some of the most important real estate in the world—the temple in Jerusalem. It was there that Jesus—the One who healed the sick, raised the dead, and was called the Prince of Peace—fashioned a whip and in an angry outburst drove the moneychangers from the temple. Staying in Jerusalem, Mart De Haan and the Jesus Study Group pay a visit to the Temple Mount to discuss this event and what it teaches us about the historical Jesus Christ.

SESSION 7

The Temple Controversy

DAYLIGHT PREVIEW

Jesus Takes on the Moneychangers

As the conflict between Jesus and the authorities of His day heated up—and as it became more and more clear that they were determined to stop Him—the events that took place in the temple on the day after his triumphal entry certainly didn't make things any easier for Him. Jesus had visited the temple the day before and "looked around at all things" (Mark 11:11). But when He came back the next day, He challenged the people who were making money in the temple courts by selling birds and animals for sacrifice. When Jesus did this, He asserted His authority and in so doing challenged the authority of the religious leaders. What can we learn from His actions? That's where Session 7 takes us.

COME TOGETHER

Icebreaker Questions

1. How much of a temper did you have as a child?

2. Jesus' anger in this story is sometimes referred to as "righteous indignation." Can you remember a time when you had that kind of appropriate and justified anger?

3. Have you ever been to the Western Wall (or Wailing Wall) at Jerusalem? If so, what was that experience like?

FINDING DAYLIGHT

Experience the Video

Feel free to jot down Video Notes as you watch the presentation by Mart De Haan and the Jesus Study Group. Use the space below for those notes.

———————————— VIDEO NOTES ————————————

What to believe about Jesus

One dramatic moment in Jesus' life

The context of the temple event

The steps of the temple area

JESUS: MAN, MESSIAH, OR MORE?

What Jesus taught the day He overturned the tables

Why Jesus' actions upset the officials

The temple itself

What was Jesus reacting to? (Old Testament references)

The importance of this place and the worship of God

WALKING IN THE DAYLIGHT

Discussion Time

DISCOVER GOD'S WORD
Discussion/Application Questions

1. The cleansing of the temple comes on the heels of the triumphal entry, in which Jesus, in effect, declared himself King. We see the

first phase of the story in Mark 11:7–11. Mark points out that Jesus returned to the temple the next day. Pick up the story again by reading Mark 11:15–18.

a. Dr. Brent Kinman notes that some might describe Jesus' actions here as "aggressive." Do you consider Jesus' actions aggressive? What other words would you use? Do you find this story unsettling to a degree?

b. Pilgrims coming to the Passover Feast needed to buy sacrificial animals and to exchange their money into the local currency to pay the annual temple tax. So why was Jesus offended by these activities?

c. How were the religious leaders robbing both the common folk economically and the temple itself of its sanctity?

d. On the other hand, why were Jesus' actions so offensive to the religious authorities?

2. Dr. Craig Evans points out, in regard to the offense of the religious authorities, that Jesus was quoting Jeremiah 7, a passage that condemns the first temple. Jeremiah prophesied to the nation of Judah in the period just before and after its destruction by the Babylonians in 586 BC. For Jesus to appeal to this passage would suggest that judgment was awaiting the temple of His day. Turn to Jeremiah 7:1–11.

   a. What kinds of sins were the people guilty of?

   b. How did Jeremiah say the people were deceiving themselves in regard to the temple?

   c. Jesus referred to verse 11, charging that the ruling priests had turned the temple into a den of robbers. How does the image of thieves feeling safe as they hide in a cave fit in with Jeremiah's message regarding the people's attitude about the temple?

3. The prophet Jeremiah delivered some stinging words to the people of Judah in verses 12–15. When the Israelites first entered the Promised Land, the tabernacle was set up at Shiloh. Jeremiah was apparently referring to buildings at Shiloh, other than the tabernacle itself, that were destroyed later by the Philistines. In verse 15, God says through

Jeremiah that He will thrust Judah into exile as He had earlier the people of Ephraim, another name for the northern kingdom of Israel.

How would Jesus' allusion to this passage, with its prophecies of the first temple's destruction and Judah's exile, further inflame the religious leaders?

4. The other Old Testament Scripture that Jesus referred to was Isaiah 56:7, which reveals God's ultimate intent for the temple. Foreigners were prohibited from worshiping at the temple, but the Messiah would change that, as we see in Isaiah 56:6–7.

   a. How was the fact that the merchants and moneychangers had set up shop in the outer court, the court of the Gentiles—the only part of the temple Gentiles could enter—preventing the temple from being a house of prayer for all nations?

   b. How do you suppose the Jewish religious leaders felt about Jesus quoting this prophecy, which said that the temple, because of the Messiah, would be called a house of prayer for all peoples?

   c. Today, how close is the church in general, and your congregation in particular, to being "a house of prayer for all nations"?

DAYLIGHT ON PRAYER

A Time to Share

1. We see, in this story, Jesus' passion for worshiping God and for what it really means to pray. How would you like to grow in the area of worship and prayer?

2. How can your brothers and sisters in this group join you in praying for your personal concerns, concerns for other individuals, or concerns for situations around the world?

DAYLIGHT AHEAD

Are you ready for a trip to the temple? First, you have to go through a purification process—and you're going to get a little wet. As Mart De Haan and the Jesus Study Group explain the process of going to the temple to worship, you'll get a first-hand look at the steps necessary to worship at the temple in Jesus' day. Dr. Klyne Snodgrass and Dr. Craig Evans will take you down into the *mikvah*—the purification pools outside the temple. In this way, they re-introduce us to the story of Jesus and the temple—and what it means in the spirit of proving the realities of Jesus' life.

SESSION 8

What Was Jesus Doing?

DAYLIGHT PREVIEW

A Threat to the Temple

Jesus took the temple seriously. So did the religious leaders of His day. However, Jesus knew something about it that they didn't seem to know. He knew how it fit in with Old Testament prophecies—that's why He quoted two passages from the ancient book. And He knew that the temple would be destroyed. While they saw it as a worship center under their jurisdiction, Jesus saw it as "My house," and He treated it as His. Both saw what was happening in the temple as a threat and acted accordingly. This is the reality of the temple controversy and Jesus' relationship to it.

COME TOGETHER

Icebreaker Questions

1. Have you ever visited a public bath or hot springs?

2. Can you recall a time when you were a victim of exorbitant exchange rates or price gouging or got a really bad deal?

3. How much of a skeptic are you by nature?

FINDING DAYLIGHT

Experience the Video

Feel free to jot down Video Notes as you watch the presentation by Mart De Haan and the Jesus Study Group. Use the space below for those notes.

---------- VIDEO NOTES ----------

The situation in the temple

Purification of the temple worshipers

What issues do scholars raise concerning this event?

What do skeptical scholars bring to the text?

    Faulty assumptions

    Theological bias

SESSION 8—What Was Jesus Doing?

Placing biblical events in context to understand Jesus

What scholars do to undermine Scripture

The temple controversy: What to do with it

Jesus' call to make disciples

Be the temple: A Christian concept

Mart's summation

WALKING IN THE DAYLIGHT

Discussion Time

---DISCOVER GOD'S WORD---

Discussion/Application Questions

1. This session begins with a look at the *mikvahs*, the ritual purification pools that were part of worshiping God at the ancient temple at Jerusalem.

   How does the presence of these purification pools stand in contrast to the commercialization that was occurring at the temple in Jesus' day?

2. **In the Synoptic Gospels (Matthew, Mark, and Luke), the cleansing of the temple takes place during the last week of Jesus' life; but in the gospel of John this event occurs early in Jesus' public ministry, right after His first miracle of changing water into wine. Perhaps there were two cleansings, both at the beginning and at the end of Jesus' ministry. Or maybe John chose to place his account at the beginning of his gospel for theological reasons—for example, to demonstrate that God's authority worked through Jesus the Messiah throughout His ministry.**

   How would you expect scholars who doubt the authenticity of this story to handle this issue?

3. As you read John 2:12–17, note that John's account includes some details that aren't found in the other Gospels: Jesus making a whip, scattering the coins of the moneychangers, and delivering a slightly different message.

   How do these things illustrate Jesus' "zeal" that the disciples later connected to Psalm 69:9, as John notes in verse 17?

4. In the accounts in the Synoptic Gospels, Jesus quotes Isaiah 56 and Jeremiah 7: "Is it not written, 'My house shall be called a house of prayer for all nations'? But you have made it a 'den of thieves' " (Mark 11:17, NKJV).

   a. Why do some scholars find it hard to believe that Jesus would appeal to Old Testament passages?

   b. How would you respond to this skepticism?

5. Dr. Craig Evans points out that about thirty years later another man by the name of Jesus—Jesus ben Ananias (Jesus, the son of Ananias)—also preached messages against the temple based on Jeremiah 7.

   What does that say about the skeptics' argument?

6. Dr. Evans believes that these critical scholars "underestimate the close linkage the Gospels have to eyewitnesses and to early apostolic teaching."

   Why is that close linkage important?

7. Dr. Michael Wilkins also sees a theological bias at work. According to the accounts in the Gospels, Jesus comes to Jerusalem knowing what is going to happen to Him and that His death is not going to be just a martyr's death but rather the sacrifice for the people of Israel—for the people of the entire world. Skeptical scholars question how Jesus could really know this. And some would say there is no such thing as that kind of atoning sacrifice.

   a. How would you respond to these kinds of arguments?

   b. The skeptical scholars focus on Jesus as a social reformer. To what extent would it be accurate to say, instead, that the crux of the issue is Jesus' authority—His almost breathtaking authority as Messiah and ruler of Israel to take control of the temple and in effect to say, "I've got a right to direct you in terms of what the worship of God ought to be"?

8. Dr. Wilkins notes that before Jesus ascended He said, "Go and make disciples of all the nations" (Matthew 28:19).

    What does the fact that the nations, the Gentiles, no longer have to come to the temple say about the person and authority of Jesus?

9. At the end of this session, Mart De Haan reflects: "Today as I walk among the merchants of modern Jerusalem, I'm reminded of how easy it would have been for me to be one of those moneychangers that angered Jesus. I've seen all too often how inclined I am to think of worship as something to be done to meet my own needs."

    Reflecting on your own life: How are you guilty of that kind of thinking?

DAYLIGHT ON PRAYER

A Time to Share

1. Dr. Klyne Snodgrass points out that in the ancient world there were no religious groups that did not have a temple with priests—except Christians. "All of a sudden they become the temple, and they don't need a priest to approach God. And so they are to embody what it means to be the temple in the way that they serve God and each other."

2. You can "be the temple" and serve each other by coming to God on each other's behalf. Spend some time "carrying each other's burdens" (Galatians 6:2) as you support and pray for one another.

DAYLIGHT AHEAD

The Last Supper. It's one of the most iconic images of the New Testament. Immortalized by Leonardo da Vinci in his famous and oft-imitated painting, this event is one we think we recognize. But as you step into an upper room with Mart De Haan, Dr. Darrel Bock, Dr. Robert Webb, and Dr. Michael Wilkins, you'll get a different picture of the scene. In Session 9 you'll join these men at the table as they examine the biblical accounts of this meal to see if it can be proved to have really happened.

SESSION 9

Jesus and the Last Supper

DAYLIGHT PREVIEW

A New Meaning

The Passover meal has been celebrated in Jewish homes for thousands of years. It is a special moment of commemorating the time when Pharaoh finally let the Jewish people leave Egypt and slavery behind under Moses' leadership. But as Jesus calls His disciples together in an upper room in Jerusalem, He is about to give new meaning to this traditional meal. And as we will see in Session 9, those who wrote down the gospel accounts understood the change that took place at the Last Supper. This meal, then, becomes another piece of evidence in the ongoing search for reason to believe that Jesus was the Messiah.

COME TOGETHER

Icebreaker Questions

1. Mart De Haan and three New Testament scholars, meeting in a room used by tourists and pilgrims to experience what the Last Supper might have been like, tried to simulate the disciples' reclining position. What unusual dining positions or places have you experienced?

2. When you were growing up, were any parts of your house (e.g., the living room) off limits for eating?

3. Have you ever participated in a Passover meal?

4. For generations, Leonardo da Vinci's painting *The Last Supper* has given people an impression of what the meal that Jesus shared with His disciples looked like. Where have you seen that, or another depiction, displayed?

FINDING DAYLIGHT

Experience the Video

Feel free to jot down Video Notes as you watch the presentation by Mart De Haan and the Jesus Study Group. Use the space below for those notes.

──────────────── **VIDEO NOTES** ────────────────

Background of the Last Supper

The context of the Last Supper

The Passover story and its remembrance

What Jesus does with the Passover

Why scholars examine the Passover

The Last Supper and Paul's letter to the Corinthians

The Last Supper and the pattern of Jesus' action

Why this meal makes sense

WALKING IN THE DAYLIGHT

Discussion Time

DISCOVER GOD'S WORD

Discussion/Application Questions

1. **The background of the Last Supper was the Jewish Passover meal. We can read about the original Passover in Exodus 12:1–14.**

   a. Why do you suppose each family's chosen lamb had to be without defect (v. 5)?

   b. How did the lambs, specifically their blood, serve as a substitute for the Israelites?

   c. Down through the ages, what would the bitter herbs (v. 8) remind the Jewish people of as they ate the Passover meal?

   d. What was the reason for the unusual instructions in verse 11? (Note: Though the meal was originally eaten while standing, in Jesus' day it was customary to eat it while reclining—the typical position at a banquet.)

2. Let's take a look now at the preparation for the Last Supper, according to Mark 14:12–16. Jesus evidently had made prior arrangements with the owner of the house to celebrate the Passover there. According to custom, those who had a room available in Jerusalem would make it available to Passover pilgrims upon request for this purpose. Judas Iscariot had gone to the chief priests to betray Jesus and was watching for an opportunity to hand Jesus over to them. By not identifying ahead of time where He would eat the Passover meal, Jesus could prevent Judas from informing the religious leaders, who might have disrupted this important event.

   The gospel of Luke adds that when Jesus and His disciples gathered at the large upper room that evening, Jesus said, "I have eagerly desired to eat this Passover with you before I suffer" (Luke 22:15). How do these preparations illustrate that strong desire?

3. Note the sad announcement that Jesus makes during the supper, recorded in Mark 14:17–21. It was customary at a meal in Jesus' day (and practiced yet today by some in the Middle East) to dip a piece of bread into a bowl of stewed fruit on the table. Eating with a person communicated a pledge of friendship and a commitment not to do that person harm.

   How does this cultural reality magnify Judas' actions?

4. **Now read the rest of Mark's account of the Last Supper in Mark 14:22–26.**

   How did Jesus change the symbolism of the Passover meal in light of what was about to take place?

5. **Some historians question whether the conversation really occurred the way Mark and the other Gospels recorded it. They suggest those words were added to the story years later in order to leave the impression that Jesus knew He was about to die and that He wanted to give the Passover meal new meaning.**

   a. How logical is this claim? How would you respond to it?

   b. How much do you think Jesus knew about what was ahead of Him and about what those events would mean?

6. **A reference to the Last Supper also appears in 1 Corinthians, one of the earliest New Testament texts—written about 25 years after Jesus' death and resurrection and perhaps even before the Gospels. Turn to 1 Corinthians 11:23–26. (Note: When Paul says in verse 23 that he received this teaching from the Lord, that doesn't necessarily**

mean that he received it directly from Christ; others who had heard it from Jesus likely passed the information on to him.)

a. In light of the skeptics' charge that the writers of the Gospels added Jesus' words about His sacrificial death to their accounts of the Last Supper, how significant is it that this account appears here in 1 Corinthians?

b. How does Paul's statement in verse 26 confirm that the early church understood that celebrating the Lord's Supper was to be an ongoing ordinance?

Reflecting on your own life: What does it mean to you, personally, that each time you take Communion you "proclaim the Lord's death until He comes"?

DAYLIGHT ON PRAYER

A Time to Share

1. What prayer concerns would you like to share with the group?

2. Conclude your prayer time by spending some time thanking God for "passing over" your sins because of the blood of Christ. Thank Him for delivering you from the bitterness of spiritual bondage through the sacrifice of His Son.

DAYLIGHT AHEAD

The team continues to recline at a table much like the one Jesus and His disciples used at the Last Supper. As they do, in addition to being very uncomfortable, they will examine such things as a connection between this story and Isaiah 53, how the meal itself fits into the whole picture of faith, and why the Lord's Supper is still significant today.

SESSION 10

Jesus Introduces His Death

DAYLIGHT PREVIEW

The Suffering Servant

The time is coming for Jesus to die. While His disciples don't have a clear idea that this is about to happen, the Last Supper is another indicator for them that what Jesus is about to do has great significance. As they meet around the table, they are about to see the unfolding of a passage of Scripture that they had heard but did not understand: Isaiah 53. At this meal, Jesus would link this event with His coming death—and He wanted this meal to be a commemoration of what He would do for people as the suffering Servant of mankind—the Savior of the world.

COME TOGETHER

Icebreaker Questions

1. What special memories do you have of family meals or gatherings when you were growing up?

2. What are some of the best potluck dinners you've been to?

3. What farewell party stands out in your memory? How sad was it?

FINDING DAYLIGHT

Experience the Video

Feel free to jot down Video Notes as you watch the presentation by Mart De Haan and the Jesus Study Group. Use the space below for those notes.

---── **VIDEO NOTES** ──---

How does the Last Supper fit into the context?

Isaiah 53 and how it fits

History of Israel and sacrifice—relating to Jesus

A new memorial

The Exodus, the Passover, and Jesus' new plan

The Last Supper as a culmination and a reflection

How this meal fits into the whole picture

What to do with the Lord's Supper

    Its significance and importance

    Its reminder of new life

    Its reminder of fellowship

WALKING IN THE DAYLIGHT

Discussion Time

---DISCOVER GOD'S WORD---

Discussion/Application Questions

1. As part of his argument that Jesus did indeed use the Passover observance in reference to His imminent death, Dr. Darrell Bock points out that Jewish literature written after the Old Testament period, such as the Fourth Book of Maccabees, shows that the Jewish people were beginning to contemplate the possibility of a righteous person dying on behalf of others, even the nation. The roots of that concept go to a text like Isaiah 53, a passage about the suffering servant—the Messiah. More than six hundred years before Jesus was born, the prophet Isaiah had foreseen a righteous servant who, like a sacrificial Passover lamb, would bear the sin of others. Read this remarkably specific description in Isaiah 53:1–12.

    a. How strongly does the idea of the suffering servant, the Messiah, dying on behalf of others come through in this passage?

    b. This servant song of Isaiah 52:13–53:12 is quoted more often in the New Testament than any other Old Testament passage. Can you see why it has been called the "gospel in the Old Testament"?

SESSION 10—Jesus Introduces His Death

2. **Luke includes material in his account of the Last Supper that isn't found in the other Gospels. Pick up the story by reading Luke 22:7–20.**

   How amazing is it that Jesus took one of the most fundamental symbols of the Jewish faith—the Exodus from Egypt—and suddenly began to talk about another kind of deliverance that was going to take place?

3. **Continue looking at Luke's account by reading Luke 22:21–34. Dr. Robert Webb notes that though the Passover meal looked back to the Exodus as God's salvation in the past, the Old Testament Prophets and other Jewish literature used the same language to talk about what the people of Israel expected God to do in the future.**

   a. How was Jesus embodying these hopes for the future in Himself, particularly as seen in verses 16, 18, and 29–30?

   b. How does this scene show how Jesus tried to prepare His disciples for what was about to happen to Him and that they needed to be ready to walk down the same kind of path—and yet how little they really understood about all of this at the time? (Note: The word "you" in verse 31 is plural, meaning that Jesus was addressing all of the disciples, not just Simon Peter.)

c. What do you think it was like for the disciples to have been at this meal and then remember and reflect later, after Jesus' death and resurrection, about what He said and what He went through?

4. **Mart De Haan asks the three scholars what they would like people to do with these ideas about the Last Supper. Dr. Michael Wilkins says: "So often we just do church; we do ceremonies; we do religious ritual. We may take Communion, the Lord's Supper, once a month, or once a year, or once a week. And yet it just becomes so trivial. Jesus descended into the hell of torture of payment of sin so that I can be free; so that I can find salvation; so that all of us can know what it means to be free in Christ. We should never trivialize the Lord's Supper by just taking a little wafer and drinking a little juice. We should basically weep and then rejoice at what Jesus meant."**

   Dr. Bock, in a sense, looks at the other side of the coin. In Communion, we remember Christ's death; He said, "You remember My death until I come again." But Communion is about a death that leads into life. "It leads into a new life for Jesus—in His resurrected form. It leads into a new life to anyone who embraces what Jesus offers. And so, as a result, sometimes when you take the Lord's Supper you have this sense of solemnity and almost a glumness on focusing on the death. Sometimes we forget that the meal is about fellowship. We forget that the meal is about life. And so it transcends that death. Jesus didn't die just to die; He died to bring life. So that is part of what's being celebrated as well."

   Reflecting on your life: How do you feel about these two men's observations? Do you tend to take the Lord's Supper for granted or too lightly? How can you prevent that?

Reflecting on your own life: What attitudes and emotions should be encouraged "whenever you eat this bread and drink this cup" (1 Corinthians 11:26)?

5. In response to Mart's question, Dr. Webb said, "In the ancient Near-Eastern world, the Mediterranean world, the Greco-Roman world, Jesus' world, when you ate together, you were in fellowship with the people you ate with. It was a sign of agreement and of oneness. For me, when I celebrate Communion, it is a celebration of my fellowship that I have with God. And I am accepted at His table."

   Reflecting on your own life: What does it mean to you to be accepted at God's "table"? Do you have that sense of acceptance right now?

DAYLIGHT ON PRAYER

A Time to Share

1. Dr. Bock points out that the Lord's Supper is a *family* meal. The intimacy and acceptance it brings is a very powerful reminder that Jesus' life and ministry was designed to invite people into fellowship with the living God. How can your brothers and sisters in this group support you in your fellowship with Him and with other believers?

2. What other matters related to the family of God around the world can you lift up to the living God together in prayer?

DAYLIGHT AHEAD

While it is not possible to walk the exact footsteps of Jesus on the night of His arrest and His appearance before the officials, it is possible to imagine how troubling that series of events was for Jesus and His followers. But did the events take place as we are told in Scripture? Mart De Haan is joined by three New Testament scholars as they sit in the courtyard of the Church of St. Peter in Gallicantu—a church built to recall that event. With a statue of Peter's denial of Jesus in the background, the men discuss evidence to support the truthfulness of the Bible's record.

SESSION 11

The Examination of Jesus

DAYLIGHT PREVIEW

A Decision That Changed The World

When Jesus was arrested and made to stand before His first accusers, those people had no power to put Him to death. Their objections were of a religious nature, and their findings could not reach the level of a capital offense. But what Jesus knew, and no one else seemed to understand, was this: for His work on earth to be accomplished, His life had to be taken—He had to be killed. That made His examination and the results of it vitally important. The decision of the Romans to get involved in this "religious" conflict—for the Jewish leaders to take the case to Pilate and for him to accept it—was vital for God's plan to be carried out. This was, we all know now, a decision that changed the world.

COME TOGETHER

Icebreaker Questions

1. Have you ever seen a bird do what the visiting feathered friend did on the set of *Day of Discovery*—fly in from out of nowhere and make a surprise visit?

2. Have you ever served on a jury or come close to being selected?

3. How involved do you get in following high-profile court cases? Or in legal dramas on TV?

FINDING DAYLIGHT

Experience the Video

Feel free to jot down Video Notes as you watch the presentation by Mart De Haan and the Jesus Study Group. Use the space below for those notes.

―――――――――― VIDEO NOTES ――――――――――

The road to the Mount of Olives

What really happened the night Jesus was led away?

The falcon, the bell, and the call to prayer

A scene that changed history: The examination

    The purpose of the inquiry

Why they had to get it right

Why was it not a trial?

The first charge: The temple

Why the effort was not successful

The high priest's question and Jesus' response

Jesus' two implications from two passages

    Psalm 110

    Daniel 7

The high priest's response and charge

WALKING IN THE DAYLIGHT

Discussion Time

DISCOVER GOD'S WORD

Discussion/Application Questions

1. **The next scene in the high drama of Jesus' "passion," or suffering, is His arrest. Look at Mark's account of this story in Mark 14:43–52.**

   a. Mark's note in verse 43 that the arresting party was sent by the chief priests, teachers of the law (or scribes), and the elders is a reference to the Sanhedrin, Israel's religious supreme court. Why do you suppose they arrested Jesus in a garden at night rather than, as Jesus asked in verses 48–49, while He was teaching in the temple?

   b. As an expression of respect, disciples customarily greeted their rabbi with a kiss. What words come to your mind as you read about Judas and Jesus in this scene?

2. **Only the gospel of Mark (verses 51–52) includes the reference to a young man at Jesus' arrest. Many believe this to be John Mark, the writer of this gospel. We know from John's gospel that Peter was the one who struck the servant of the high priest with a sword, and we know from Luke's gospel that Jesus touched and healed the man's ear. Jesus' statement in verse 49 about the Scriptures being fulfilled was likely a reference to Zechariah 13:7, which Jesus had quoted while speaking to the disciples earlier that evening, as recorded in Mark 14:27. Read Mark 14:27–31.**

   Although Jesus tried to prepare Peter and the other disciples for what was about to happen, why do you think they responded the way they did?

3. **Continue Mark's narrative by reading Mark 14:53–59.**

   a. Why was Jesus' appearance before the Sanhedrin an "examination" rather than a "trial"? What was the Sanhedrin's objective?

   b. What does Dr. Darrell Bock mean when he says that the fact that the Jewish leaders didn't have the authority to put Jesus to death provided a cover for them?

   c. What specific accusation was made against Jesus? Why was that something the Romans would take very seriously?

4. **The testimony quoted in verse 58 is probably a reference to Jesus' conversation with the religious leaders as reported in John's account of Jesus cleansing the temple. Turn to John 2:18–22.**

   What did Jesus mean about destroying the temple and raising it again in three days? How would that prove His authority to drive the merchants and moneychangers out of the temple?

5. **The Sanhedrin's effort to bring a charge or secure an indictment was unsuccessful up to this point because they couldn't get the witnesses to agree. Pick up the story again by reading Mark 14:60–65.**

   a. How did both the high priest and Jesus use, as Dr. Bock points out, a circumlocution—in other words, speaking around the name of God, referring to God without pronouncing His name?

   b. Why did Jesus' words make the high priest and the rest of the Sanhedrin so angry? Why did they consider what He said to be blasphemy?

DAYLIGHT ON PRAYER

A Time to Share

1. Combining portions of Psalm 110:1 and Daniel 7:13, Jesus was claiming, in Mark 14:62, to be exalted, to have all authority, and to be the future and ultimate Judge. What impact do those claims have on your life?

2. What prayer requests would you like to share with the group?

3. Conclude your prayer time by praising Jesus, the Exalted One—acknowledging and honoring His power and authority.

DAYLIGHT AHEAD

You've heard about the Sanhedrin—that group of men in Jesus' day who ruled on Jewish law in the lives of the people. But did you know that a revitalized Sanhedrin exists today in Israel? In Session 12, you'll get a first-hand look at their current activities as Mart De Haan and some of the scholars from the Jesus Study Group work through the facts of the examination of Jesus, first by the Sanhedrin and later by Pontius Pilate. As they do, they will take a close look at the objections that have been raised by those who don't think this examination of Jesus happened as the Bible says it did.

SESSION 12

Objections to the Examination Story

DAYLIGHT PREVIEW

It Makes Sense

At the crux of the Christian faith is the idea that Jesus Christ stood before Pontius Pilate, was sentenced to die, and was crucified for our sins. The serious contemplation of these facts by thoughtful, diligent people is not a danger to the truthfulness of the story, as Dr. Michael Wilkins, Dr. Darrell Bock, and Dr. Craig Evans make clear in their discussion of the topic. As Dr. Bock says, "It makes sense." It makes sense historically because the facts of the story can be supported, and it makes sense spiritually because the result of the story has implications for every person on earth. It might seem like a dangerous thing to put the story of Jesus on trial and ask tough questions about it—but it can stand the examination because it makes sense.

COME TOGETHER

Icebreaker Questions

1. How good are you at figuring out the culprit in a "Who done it?" plot?

2. Dr. Darrell Bock mentions the "Jerusalem grapevine." What grapevine(s) are you tapped into?

3. Who was your hero when you were a child? Though Peter became a hero in the early church, he didn't look like a hero in this story. Have you ever been disappointed by a hero?

FINDING DAYLIGHT

Experience the Video

Feel free to jot down Video Notes as you watch the presentation by Mart De Haan and the Jesus Study Group. Use the space below for those notes.

―――――――――― VIDEO NOTES ――――――――――

The present-day Sanhedrin

The ancient Sanhedrin and Jesus' examination

Josephus' response to that argument

Another objection: The people who cared weren't there

The context of the events

Dr. Bock's story

Staying open to the possibilities

Historical and personal sense of the story

Peter's denial and historicity

Josephus' corroboration

Mart's summation

WALKING IN THE DAYLIGHT

Discussion Time

DISCOVER GOD'S WORD

Discussion/Application Questions

1. The Jesus Study Group scholars address two objections to the historical authenticity of the Gospels' accounts of the examination of Jesus. Some scholars say the Sanhedrin, Israel's religious supreme court, could not have been involved in the interrogation because to do so they would have had to break the rules of their own council regarding trials deciding life and death. They point to discrepancies between what is laid out in the Mishnah, a collection of Jewish oral traditions put into writing more than a hundred years after Jesus' lifetime, and what takes place in Jerusalem according to the Gospels.

   Dr. Craig Evans counters that the first-century Jewish historian Josephus tells us that the ruling priests broke the rules all the time. Dr. Darrell Bock adds that the Sanhedrin was rushing to get to Pilate and that this was an examination rather than a capital murder trial, which was the context of the Mishnah. Dr. Bock dismisses this debate as a rabbit trail or cul-de-sac. In what ways do you agree?

2. The other objection is that since none of the disciples were present at the hearing, the report about it could not have possibly gotten into the Gospels—and therefore these accounts must be a later invention. Dr. Bock responds that there were many possible sources for getting this information, particularly Nicodemus and Joseph of Arimathea,

who were members of the Sanhedrin. Read about them and their roles in John 3:1–2, John 19:38–39, and Luke 23:50–51.

    a. It could be argued that Nicodemus and Joseph couldn't have been present at Jesus' examination because Mark 14:64 says that "they all condemned him as worthy of death" (NIV). Does it really matter if Nicodemus and Joseph weren't present? Would the word still spread through the "grapevine"?

    b. Do you think the Sanhedrin would have preferred to keep their charges against Jesus a secret or to have them publicized?

3. **Dr. Bock also points out that the first-century historian Josephus, who was a Jew himself, recorded that Jesus was crucified by Pontius Pilate at the instigation of the Jewish leadership.**

   How significant is it that the Sanhedrin's role is corroborated outside the Bible?

4. **Another dynamic that the Jesus Study Group scholars see as confirmation of the credibility of the Gospels' accounts of the examination of Jesus is the description of Peter denying Jesus, as found in Mark 14:66–72. (Note: Verse 70 indicates that Peter's accent revealed that**

he was from Galilee, which prompted the Judeans in the courtyard to suspect he was a follower of Jesus.)

    a. Dr. Evans observes that while Jesus is inside being interrogated by the Sanhedrin, Peter is outside being intimidated by a woman. How does the fact that this woman is a servant girl, no less, add to the irony and embarrassment?

    b. Why does this story not make sense as fiction—or, as Dr. Evans describes it, as "the stuff of pious imagination"?

5. Dr. Bock shares some of his own journey of coming to believe in the Bible, specifically these passages about Jesus. He states that the Bible makes historical sense, and it also makes personal sense. It helps us define who we are as people.

Why does the story of Jesus' examination in particular and the gospel in general make sense to you?

6. Mart De Haan asks: "If somebody says, 'But I just don't have your faith,' how do you respond?" Dr. Bock replies, "I think the main thing is to stay open. Don't close your mind to the possibility. Because what is on the other side of this possibility will be a redefining of what life and existence really is and what it means to be connected to God, to the creation, to life, to understanding life and death. Jesus died not to die—He died to bring life."

Reflecting on your own life: What questions do you hear from others who doubt? How can you help them?

DAYLIGHT ON PRAYER

A Time to Share

1. Peter, perhaps more than anyone else in the Bible, is known for his highs and lows. In terms of your emotions and outlook, are you feeling high, low, or pretty mellow right now? How about in terms of your relationship with Christ?

2. How can the group support you in prayer?

3. What other prayer concerns can you share with the group?

DAYLIGHT AHEAD

Session 13 starts with a remarkable statement by Mart De Haan. "This is... Jerusalem, where... the best Man who ever lived was tortured and killed in the most cruel of executions." In Jerusalem, Mart meets with Dr. Robert Webb, Dr. Darrell Bock, and Dr. Craig Evans to discuss why Jesus was killed and what evidence we have that the story we have been told about Jesus' death was indeed accurate and true.

SESSION 13

Who Killed Jesus and Why?

DAYLIGHT PREVIEW

Wrongly Accused

Have you ever been wrongly accused? It's a helpless feeling, isn't it? Try to imagine how Jesus must have felt as He stood before Pilate. He not only knew that He had never sinned, but He also knew that God's will was for Him to be crucified. That's why His agony had been so intense in the Garden of Gethsemane. And now, as He stood before Pilate, He knew that defending himself would not only do no good but it would also be counteracting what He realized had to take place. And He understood that when He acknowledged to Pilate that the title "King of the Jews" was accurate, this admission would be just what Roman officials were looking for. This important event in the Jesus story is what Mart De Haan, Dr. Robert Webb, Dr. Darrell Bock, and Dr. Craig Evans are discussing in this session as they stand on the grounds of the Tower of David in Jerusalem.

COME TOGETHER

Icebreaker Questions

1. Mart De Haan notes that it seems like whenever he visits the Tower of David construction is going on. What place or road seems that way to you?

2. Rome maintained peace in the empire by bullying and intimidating its subjects. Who was the bully in your life when you were growing up?

3. Dr. Craig Evans points out that Pilate had a very difficult decision to make. What is one of the most difficult decisions you have ever had to make?

FINDING DAYLIGHT

Experience the Video

Feel free to jot down Video Notes as you watch the presentation by Mart De Haan and the Jesus Study Group. Use the space below for those notes.

— VIDEO NOTES —

Jesus before Pilate

The Tower of David

Crucifixion

    Public example

Frequency

What crimes?

Why was Jesus crucified?

Sedition

Offenses to Jews; Offenses to Rome

What should Pilate do?

Pilate asks the people what they wanted

WALKING IN THE DAYLIGHT

Discussion Time

DISCOVER GOD'S WORD
Discussion/Application Questions

1. We have been following Mark's account of the last events of Jesus' life in many of our recent sessions. Pick up the action by reading Mark 15:1–2. Although verse 1 may simply recap the ruling of the Sanhedrin that fateful night, it is more likely that Mark was recounting a brief second meeting. If that is the case, the decision of the first council was simply being confirmed by the whole Sanhedrin, since a legal verdict could be rendered only after daylight. At any rate, verse 2 indicates that the Sanhedrin charged Jesus before Pilate with claiming to be a king.

   Why didn't the Jewish leaders charge Jesus with blasphemy, as they had determined according to Mark 14:64?

2. We see in Mark 15:3 that the Jewish leaders accused Jesus before Pilate of many things. The gospel of Luke provides more information about these charges. Read Luke 23:1–5.

   The first charge was that Jesus was "subverting our nation," likely in the sense of turning the Jewish people against Rome. Was there any truth to that charge?

3. **The second charge was that Jesus had opposed paying taxes to Caesar (Rome). Turn to Luke 20:20–26 and see how Jesus had dealt with this issue.**

   Was there any truth to the Sanhedrin's second charge? What was Jesus' position regarding these taxes?

4. **The third charge was that Jesus claimed to be the Christ, or Messiah—a king.**

   a. Why was that the charge that evidently concerned Pilate the most?

   b. Was there any truth to that charge from Jesus' perspective? Was there any truth to the charge based on how Pilate would have perceived it?

5. **At this point, we get more information about the conversation between Pilate and Jesus from the gospel of John. Read John 18:33–40.**

   a. How did Jesus address Pilate's perception of what it meant for Jesus to be a "king"?

   b. What effect did that have on Pilate's thinking?

6. **Continue with John's account by reading John 19:1–16.**

   a. How do you see Pilate, as Dr. Bock notes, feeling a bit cornered by the Jewish leadership?

   b. What do the chief priests' ironic words in verse 18, "We have no king but Caesar," reveal about their spiritual state?

7. How would you answer the question "Why was Jesus crucified?"—according to historical circumstances? How would you answer the question "Why was Jesus crucified?"—according to God's great plan?

DAYLIGHT ON PRAYER

A Time to Share

1. What prayer requests would you like to share for yourself, your family, your friends, or situations around the world that are on your heart?

2. Focus some of your time in prayer together upon Jesus' sacrificial death on our behalf—thanking Him and renewing your allegiance and commitment to Him.

DAYLIGHT AHEAD

Standing outside the Tower of David in Jerusalem and surrounded by the old walls of the Holy City, you'll visit with Mart De Haan as he discusses with Dr. Craig Evans, Dr. Darrell Bock, and Dr. Robert Webb the examination of Jesus by Pilate. You'll listen as these scholars discuss what skeptics say about the historicity of Jesus' crucifixion—and the reason for His execution. You'll hear what these men have discovered through their extensive studies of this seminal event in history.

SESSION 14

The Reality of the Crucifixion Accounts

DAYLIGHT PREVIEW

How Did It Happen?

Could it be that Jesus' death was not what we think it was? For example, some people who have studied the history of Jesus' day say that He was simply caught up in a riot and killed inadvertently. That's just one theory the scholars of the Jesus Study Group have heard over the years as they have sought to find evidence for the truthfulness of the biblical account. In Session 14, those scholars discuss why they are confident—and why we can be just as confident—that the skeptics are wrong and the Bible is right.

COME TOGETHER

Icebreaker Questions

1. Jesus was guilty, in a sense, of "disturbing the peace." How guilty of that were you as a teenager?

2. Pilate was responsible to ensure that the peace was kept. Who made sure the peace was kept in your family when you were growing up? What tactics did that person use?

3. We might wonder why Jesus didn't try harder to defend himself. How quick were you to defend yourself as a kid? What was your typical strategy: verbal defense? Physical defense?

4. How quick are you to defend yourself now?

FINDING DAYLIGHT

Experience the Video

Feel free to jot down Video Notes as you watch the presentation by Mart De Haan and the Jesus Study Group. Use the space below for those notes.

———————— VIDEO NOTES ————————

The Tower of David

Golgotha

Pilate's historical role in Jesus' crucifixion

Alternative views of Jesus' crucifixion

Jesus was caught up in a riot

Jesus was going after Rome—a political challenge

The Jewish leadership's point of view

Why didn't Jesus defend himself?

Why did Jesus allow this to happen?

Jesus' claim on *everybody*

A message for searchers

Mart's summation

WALKING IN THE DAYLIGHT

Discussion Time

DISCOVER GOD'S WORD
Discussion/Application Questions

1. Some scholars take exception to the accounts of the Gospels regarding Jesus' crucifixion. Some believe that Jesus was crucified but that He likely got swept up in some kind of riot or general Roman crucifixion exercise. The basis for that view, according to Dr. Craig Evans, is that these scholars are skeptical that Jesus' crucifixion had anything to do with His message.

   How would you respond to that view of Jesus' crucifixion?

2. Another alternative view to the Gospels' accounts of Jesus' crucifixion is that Jesus was actually going after Rome—challenging the empire politically.

   a. How would you respond to that scenario for why Jesus was crucified?

   b. What does Dr. Darrell Bock mean when he says that, although what Jesus is doing and what He is about did threaten the structure of things in the society, "it's not a direct attack on Rome—it's much bigger"?

3. **Turn to Matthew's account of Jesus before Pilate and read Matthew 27:11–14.**

   Why do you think Jesus didn't try harder to defend himself?

4. **Go back a bit in Matthew's gospel and read Matthew 26:36–39.**

   How does this scene help to answer the question why didn't Jesus try harder to defend himself?

5. **Look now at Luke's account of the crucifixion in Luke 23:32–43.**

   a. In verse 41, how does the second criminal speak for all of us?

   b. How do Jesus' words in verse 43 demonstrate that His death was for *everyone*?

   Reflecting on your own life: How are the events of Jesus' life, death, and resurrection not just *His* story but the central theme of *your* story as well?

DAYLIGHT ON PRAYER

A Time to Share

1. Dr. Bock's encouragement to someone who is searching is to consider the difference between a religious faith that says, "I have to do it the old-fashioned way—I have to earn it," versus a religious faith that says, "God is gracious and God gives you a gift." How can you relate to both of those perspectives in your spiritual journey?

2. Dr. Bock points out that switching gears between these two perspectives can be difficult, but with the switching of gears comes a whole set of provisions. One of those is a community. How has the community of believers in general, and this group in particular, been a gift of provision to you?

3. What prayer concerns would you like to share with the group?

DAYLIGHT AHEAD

Nobody likes to talk about death. But in the Bible account, we know that it is necessary to discuss it in regard to Jesus. In Session 15, you will learn about the burial customs of Jewish families in Jesus' day. As you do and you see what generally took place when a death occurred, you'll gain a better understanding of the biblical account. In this session, you'll visit a first-century grave to get that new perspective.

SESSION 15

What Happened to Jesus' Body?

DAYLIGHT PREVIEW

The Empty Tomb

Generally speaking, dead people stay dead. Yet Christianity holds at its center the idea that its founder—its heartbeat, its Savior—broke that pattern and emerged alive from His first-century, rock-hewn grave. That single fact, debated by some, doubted by others, and embraced by all who call themselves Christians, is what brings Mart De Haan, Dr. Darrell Bock, Dr. Grant Osborne, and Dr. Craig Evans to the ruins of Herod's palace. As they sit atop what once was a first-century burial spot for Herod's family, they discuss the evidence that can help us all see why we can believe with confidence that the place where Jesus was laid after His crucifixion became an empty tomb just three days later when He walked out of it.

COME TOGETHER

Icebreaker Questions

1. Whose funeral is the first one you can remember? How did it affect you?

2. What memories do you have of Easter when you were a child?

3. Do you practice any particular Easter traditions now?

FINDING DAYLIGHT

Experience the Video

Feel free to jot down Video Notes as you watch the presentation by Mart De Haan and the Jesus Study Group. Use the space below for those notes.

———————————— VIDEO NOTES ————————————

The resurrection: The crowning event

Jewish burial traditions

Visiting the burial grounds of Herod's family

Jesus' death at Passover

Paul's point: No resurrection, no gospel

The Bible's description: Missing elements

The simple story makes it believable

Incidental details point to historicity

The disciples didn't die for a lie

WALKING IN THE DAYLIGHT

Discussion Time

DISCOVER GOD'S WORD

Discussion/Application Questions

1. Let's look at the account of Jesus' resurrection according to the gospel of Luke, beginning with Jesus' burial. Read Luke 23:50–24:1.

    Dr. Craig Evans explains that when a person died in the days of Jesus, the body was washed, perfumed, wrapped, and then taken to the family vault the very day of death. The women who are named in Luke 24:10 brought spices in order to anoint Jesus' body and grieve quietly at His tomb.

    How does the fact that the women were following normal burial practices support the credibility of Jesus' resurrection?

2. **Read Luke 24:2–8 to find out what happened when the women arrived at the tomb.**

   How does the fact that women, who weren't typically allowed to be witnesses, were the first to testify of Jesus' resurrection help verify the authenticity of His resurrection?

3. **Find out what the women did next by reading Luke 24:9–12. (Note: Verse 12 mentions Peter running to the tomb, but we know from verse 24 that Peter wasn't the only one to go to the tomb. And we know from John 20:1–9 that John outran Peter and got to the tomb first.)**

   How does the skepticism of the disciples substantiate the credibility of Jesus' resurrection?

4. **Dr. Darrell Bock points out that we don't actually get a description of Jesus' resurrection. We read, rather, of an empty tomb and of Jesus' appearances after His resurrection.**

   a. Why is that significant?

   b. How does the simplicity of the gospel accounts, with their lack of detailed events, actually validate the historicity of those accounts?

c. How do you think the early Christians would have described Jesus' resurrection if they were making it up?

5. **First Corinthians 15 is a key New Testament passage about Jesus' resurrection. See how the apostle Paul began his extended discussion in 1 Corinthians 15:1–8. (Note: Jesus' appearance to Paul himself, mentioned in verse 8, occurred on the road to Damascus several years after the resurrection, making Paul's entrance into the group of apostles unique.)**

   Other than a similar terse statement in Luke 24:34, verse 5 is the only place the Scriptures refer to Jesus appearing to Peter shortly after His resurrection. Since "all the apostles" are mentioned in verse 7, this James is surely the half-brother of Jesus, who later became a key leader of the church at Jerusalem, rather than either of the two disciples named James. Although this James didn't even believe in Jesus before the resurrection (John 7:5), he joined the band of believers after the resurrection (Acts 1:14). The brief statement here in verse 7 is the only biblical reference to the risen Christ appearing to James; nothing more about that encounter is included in the New Testament.

   How does the fact that we don't have detailed accounts of Jesus appearing to these two pillars of the church support the validity of His resurrection?

6. Some in the church at Corinth believed that Christ was raised from the dead but didn't believe that His followers would experience a physical resurrection. Paul responds to that notion in 1 Corinthians 15:12–19.

   a. What series of implications does Paul draw from the view that there is no resurrection of the dead?

   b. What does Paul's remarkable statement in verse 19 mean?

   c. How does this passage illustrate that the resurrection of Christ is what Christianity is all about?

DAYLIGHT ON PRAYER

A Time to Share

Mart De Haan concludes this session by noting that history doesn't tell us about people who have been willing to die for a lie. But it does tell us about a lot of people, like Jesus' first disciples, who have died for their beliefs. And what distinguished the disciples from others is that they didn't just die for a belief; they died for their claim to have seen, heard, and touched Jesus after His resurrection.

1. How does your faith and commitment compare to the disciples'?

2. How do you wish your faith and commitment were different? How can the group pray for you in this regard?

3. What other prayer requests would you like to share?

DAYLIGHT AHEAD

Suppose you were to make up a story about a friend who you say had died but came back to life. How would you tell it? As you will see in Session 16 of this study, you probably wouldn't tell it the way the Gospels tell of Jesus' resurrection. We will see that the gospel account of Jesus' reappearance is full of skepticism and unbelief—even from His own people. You'll be fascinated as you hear Dr. Darrell Bock, Dr. Grant Osborne, and Dr. Craig Evans tell why the story as the Scripture tells it is evidence of its authenticity. And as followers of Jesus Christ, isn't that what you need as you stake your eternal life on faith in Him?

SESSION 16

What About the Empty Tomb?

DAYLIGHT PREVIEW

Myth or Miracle?

Let's face it. The story that we center our lives and our faith around as Christians is considered by many people to be a myth. These folks just cannot bring themselves to accept the premise that a man who was declared by the government to be officially dead could spring back to life. So they call it a myth. But we, backed up by Scripture and God's leading, call it a miracle. Scholars Dr. Darrell Bock, Dr. Grant Osborne, and Dr. Craig Evans have spent years studying this vital New Testament story, and they are convinced that the evidence says it really happened as the Bible says it did. This, then, is an important study for all believers in Jesus, for it solidifies for us the reality of this most vital Bible story.

COME TOGETHER

Icebreaker Questions

1. What is one area or topic in which you could be labeled a "skeptic"?

2. When Jesus was crucified, the disciples' hopes and dreams were dashed. What hope or dream have you had to let die (at least up until now)?

3. What is one of your favorite "comeback" stories? (Feel free to share a story from your own life.)

FINDING DAYLIGHT

Experience the Video

Feel free to jot down Video Notes as you watch the presentation by Mart De Haan and the Jesus Study Group. Use the space below for those notes.

―――――――――――― **VIDEO NOTES** ――――――――――――

The disciples and the resurrection

Why it's not a myth

    Judaism and resurrection at the end

    Jesus and His followers suffered in a slow movement

    Details of Jesus' burial

    Thomas' doubt

What about doubting scholars?

Discrepancies: How are those handled?

Ceilings of disbelief

What the doubter should do

Mart at the Garden Tomb

WALKING IN THE DAYLIGHT

Discussion Time

---**DISCOVER GOD'S WORD**---

Discussion/Application Questions

1. In Session 15 we looked at the account of Jesus' resurrection according to the gospel of Luke. The next passage in Luke 24 tells us about two followers of Jesus who were walking from Jerusalem to Emmaus

on Easter Sunday. We know from verse 33 that they weren't members of Jesus' inner circle of disciples. Only one of them, Cleopas (verse 18), is named, and we know nothing more about him. Read the first part of the story in Luke 24:13–24.

    a. Verse 16 indicates that God prevented the two disciples from recognizing Jesus. Why do you think He did that?

    b. And why do you suppose Jesus asked His questions in verses 17 and 19, since He obviously knew all about the events they were discussing?

2. **Mart De Haan notes that the Gospels don't hide the doubts and unbelief of the disciples and that reports of an empty tomb didn't change their grief and despair.**

    a. How do you see that in this story?

    b. How does that argue for the credibility of the gospel accounts in regard to Jesus' resurrection?

3. **Luke 24:21 demonstrates that the two disciples expected Jesus, as the Messiah, to defeat the Romans and usher in God's kingdom. Dr. Grant Osborne points out that Jesus came not as a conquering king but to suffer—and that His followers followed Him in that suffering.**

   What does Dr. Osborne mean when he says that the Christian movement moved incredibly slowly rather than in a massive movement of victory and that this confirms that the gospel accounts of the resurrection could not have just been made up?

4. **Pick up the story in Luke again by reading Luke 24:25–35.**

   What do you think was involved in the two disciples' eyes being opened so that they could recognize Jesus?

5. **Read what happens next in Luke 24:36–43.**

   a. How does the disciples' reaction show that they had no expectations of Jesus' resurrection? And, again, how does that reality actually verify the historicity of the accounts of the resurrection?

   b. Why would Jesus want to eat food in the disciples' presence?

6. Dr. Darrell Bock says that the first Christians could have saved themselves a lot of trouble by creating a story that would have fit into the Jewish background very nicely—a story that simply said, "At the end, God is going to raise everybody and Jesus is going to be in charge."

   How does the fact that the first Christians didn't do that support the authenticity of Jesus' physical resurrection?

7. John tells us about Jesus' appearing to His disciples again a week later. Thomas wasn't there the first time, but he was this time. Read John 20:24–29.

   What do you think about Dr. Osborne's observation that Thomas' attitude, "I know all of you say you've seen Him, but I refuse to believe until I can actually touch Him," is incredibly realistic—too realistic to have been made up?

8. Darrell Bock observes that there is a key worldview issue in regard to skepticism about Jesus' resurrection. This worldview, simply, is that dead people stay dead.

   a. How is that worldview like a "ceiling" that is put on the discussion?

   b. How much do you sense that ceiling affecting people today?

c. How has Jesus crashed through that ceiling?

DAYLIGHT ON PRAYER

A Time to Share

1. How can you personally relate to Thomas' doubts and skepticism?

2. How can you personally relate to Thomas' shift in faith and allegiance to Jesus?

3. How can the group support you and pray for your relationship with Jesus—your Lord and your God (John 20:28)—in the days ahead?